REPTILES

PARTS OF AN
ANIMAL

Written by Emilie Dufresne

BookLife
PUBLISHING

©2018
Book Life
King's Lynn
Norfolk PE30 4LS

ISBN: 978-1-78637-435-6

Written by:
Emilie Dufresne

Edited by:
Kirsty Holmes

Designed by:
Amy Li

REPTILES

Words that look like **this** can be found in the glossary on page 24.

WHAT IS A REPTILE?

There are so many animals in the world that we split them into different **categories**. This helps us tell all of the animals apart.

One of these categories is reptiles.

Corn Snake

Stegosaurus

Tortoise

There are lots of different types of reptiles, such as snakes, lizards, turtles, crocodiles, and even dinosaurs!

HOW DO YOU KNOW?

We can ask certain questions to find out if an animal is a reptile or not.

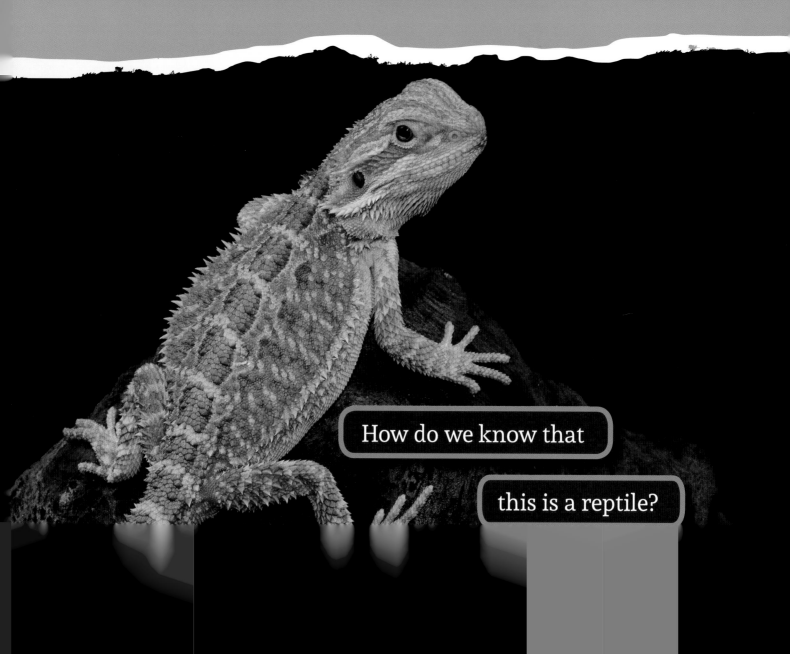

How do we know that

this is a reptile?

CHECKLIST

Does it have a backbone? ✓

Is it covered in scales or **scutes**? ✓

Does it lay hard-shelled eggs? ✓

Is it cold-blooded? ✓

IT'S A REPTILE!

HEADS AND SHOULDERS

Lots of reptiles have heads and shoulders like humans.
It's their necks that are interesting...

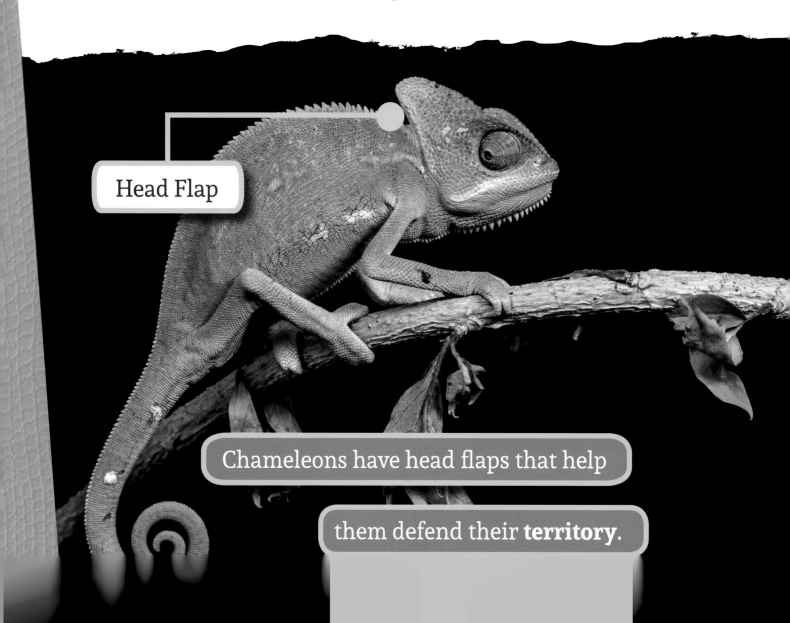

Head Flap

Chameleons have head flaps that help

them defend their **territory**.

Cobras are a type of snake. A cobra can create a hood around its neck by spreading its ribs flat. Cobras do this to seem bigger, and scare **predators**.

KNEES AND TOES

If a reptile has legs (some don't!), their knees are much like human knees. Their toes are very different...

Geckos have lots of tiny hairs on their toes to help them climb.

The thorny devil is a lizard that can soak up water through tiny grooves in its feet. This water travels up its skin and into its mouth.

EYES AND EARS

This chameleon has amazing eyes. He can see in two directions at once. His vision is **panoramic**.

Snake – No Ears

Lizard – Ear **Membranes**

Snakes don't have ears. Instead they hear by feeling different vibrations through the ground. Lizards have membranes that transfer sounds to their inner ears.

MOUTH AND NOSE

Reptile mouths are all different.

Some have really long tongues.

Some have teeth.

Some have no teeth.

Snakes' tongues work with their noses. Their tongues pick up smell **particles** and transfer them to the snake's nose. This helps it catch prey and stay away from predators.

SKIN

A reptile's skin is made from the same thing as human hair and nails. Many people think that reptiles would feel slimy, when really they feel dry.

Some reptiles feel smooth and some feel rough.

Some geckos eat the skin they shed.

WELL... THAT'S DINNER SORTED!

Certain reptiles shed their skin every so often. This helps the reptile grow and heal any wounds it might have.

17

REPTILES THAT BREAK THE RULES

If this gecko is being attacked, it can detach

its tail to get away. Afterwards, it grows a new tail.

Boa constrictors can have a **litter** of up to 15 babies.

Most snakes produce eggs that hatch baby snakes. Boa constrictors are one of a few reptiles who give birth to live young.

RADICAL REPTILES

This is the Spider-Man lizard. If it feels threatened, its skin turns bright red and blue.

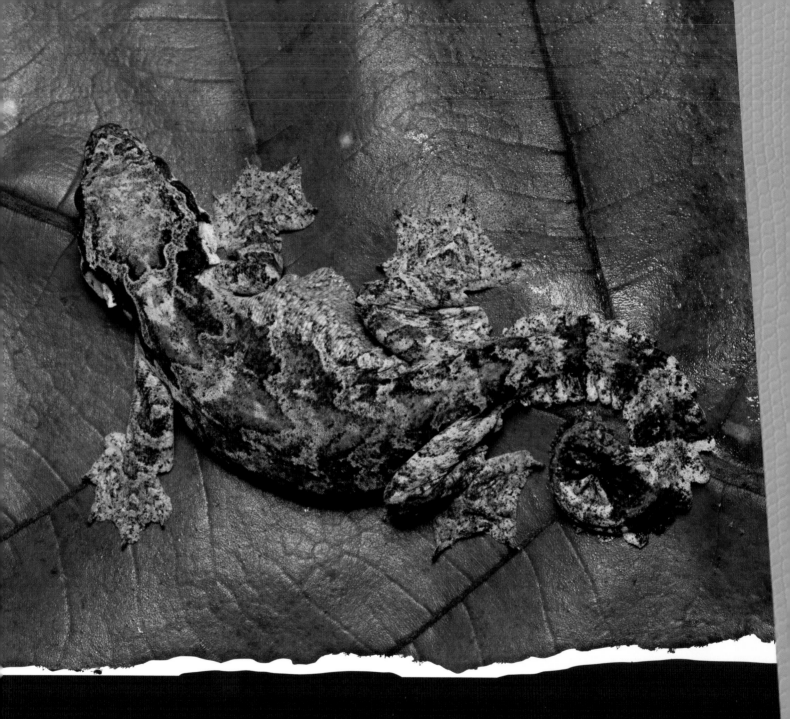

This is the flying gecko. They have **concealed** flaps of skin that open when they jump from a tree and help them glide.

ACTIVITY

Design your own reptile. What type of reptile will you choose?
What colour will it be? Will it have any special features?
What will you call it?

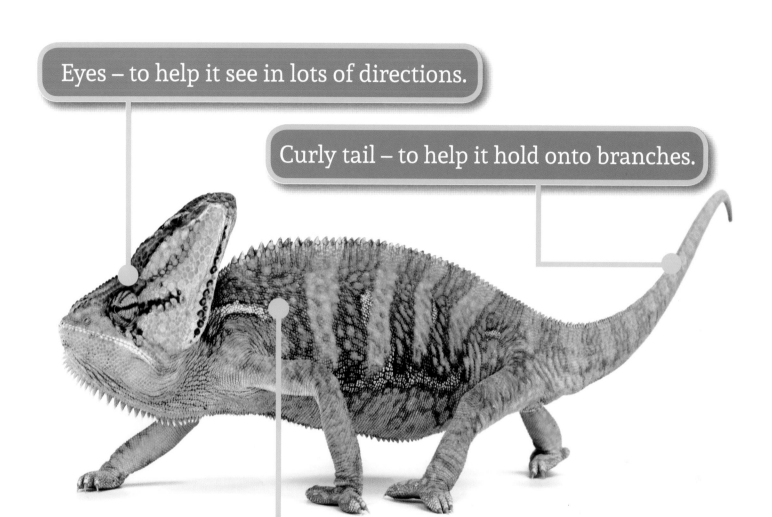

Eyes – to help it see in lots of directions.

Curly tail – to help it hold onto branches.

Colour-changing skin – to **camouflage** it.

Label your drawing with all the amazing features it has.
How do these features help the reptile?

GLOSSARY

CAMOUFLAGE	traits that allow an animal to hide itself in a habitat
CATEGORIES	different sections within a larger group
CONCEALED	hidden from sight
LITTER	a group of young animals that were born at the same time and all have one mother
MEMBRANES	a thin, soft, flexible layer that vibrates when sound waves strike it
PANORAMIC	to be able to see a large area
PARTICLES	extremely small pieces of a substance
PREDATORS	animals that hunt other animals for food
SCUTES	thick horns or scales that grow on reptiles
TERRITORY	an area that a particular animal claims as its own

INDEX